Charles Manson (1934-2017) - An American Cult Leader and Criminal Mastermind

Scarlett Prescott

Published by Serene Publishing House, 2023.

While every precaution has been taken in the preparation of this book, the publisher assumes no responsibility for errors or omissions, or for damages resulting from the use of the information contained herein.

CHARLES MANSON (1934-2017) - AN AMERICAN CULT LEADER AND CRIMINAL MASTERMIND

First edition. August 1, 2023.

ISBN: 979-8223725039

Written by Scarlett Prescott.

Table of Contents

Chapter 1: Early Life and Troubled Childhood

Charles Manson was born on November 12, 1934, in Cincinnati, Ohio, to Kathleen Maddox, a 16-year-old single mother. Manson's early family life was marked by instability and challenges. His mother struggled with various issues, including alcoholism and petty criminal activities.

Kathleen was unable to provide a stable environment for Charles, leading to a turbulent childhood. She was in and out of prison, leaving young Charles in the care of relatives and strangers for extended periods. As a result, he experienced neglect and lacked the nurturing that is crucial for healthy emotional development.

The absence of a stable family and positive role models contributed to Charles Manson's early behavioral issues. At a young age, he showed signs of aggression and delinquency, often engaging in petty theft and truancy. He frequently ran away from home, seeking a sense of belonging and purpose elsewhere.

By the time Manson reached his early teenage years, his behavior had escalated, and he found himself in and out of juvenile detention centers. These early encounters with the law foreshadowed the criminal path he would follow in his later life.

The challenging upbringing, lack of parental guidance, and exposure to criminality played a significant role in shaping Charles Manson's personality and worldview. These early experiences would eventually contribute to his transformation into a cult leader and criminal mastermind, with a notorious reputation that would make an indelible mark on American history.

Charles Manson's troubled childhood continued to be characterized by neglect and criminality. After being repeatedly abandoned by his mother, he was placed in the care of various relatives and institutions. These unstable living arrangements further fueled his feelings of rejection and fueled his delinquent behavior.

As Manson entered his teenage years, his criminal activities escalated. He was involved in several burglaries and auto thefts, landing him in juvenile detention centers multiple times. During his incarcerations, he became acquainted with seasoned criminals and started to learn the ways of a criminal lifestyle.

The lack of a stable family environment and a series of adverse experiences left Charles Manson searching for a sense of belonging and purpose. In his early teens, he started to experiment with drugs, which further compounded his behavioral issues.

At the age of 17, Manson was released from a detention center and tried to live a conventional life. He married Rosalie Willis and fathered a son, but his inability to provide for his family led to more run-ins with the law. Eventually, he was arrested for the theft of a car and sent to prison.

Prison life would become a significant part of Manson's early adulthood. While incarcerated, he began to study various self-help books, philosophy, and even learned to play the guitar. These pursuits, however, were not enough to rehabilitate him. Instead, they became tools for manipulating and captivating others, skills he would later employ as the leader of his infamous cult, the Manson Family.

The early life of Charles Manson was marred by a combination of neglect, criminal behavior, and a yearning for identity and purpose. These formative years laid the groundwork for the emergence of a charismatic yet malevolent figure, whose actions would come to define him as an American cult leader and criminal mastermind.

As Charles Manson progressed into his late teens and early adulthood, the signs of his troubled psyche became more evident. His experiences with neglect and criminality had deeply affected his emotional and mental well-being, leading to increasingly erratic and violent behavior.

In 1951, Manson's criminal activities reached a new level when he committed a series of armed robberies. These actions culminated in his arrest and subsequent conviction. At the age of 17, he was sentenced to reform school but quickly escalated to more serious institutions due to his continued aggressive and unruly conduct.

During his time in prison, Manson's manipulative nature and charismatic demeanor became apparent. He had a knack for drawing in fellow inmates and earning their admiration, often leading them to commit acts of violence on his behalf. This early display of leadership and control over others foreshadowed his future role as the leader of the Manson Family.

Manson's time in prison also fueled his growing resentment towards society and authority figures. He developed a deep-seated belief that the world had wronged him, and he sought retribution through acts of violence and rebellion. This burgeoning hostility laid the groundwork for the darker aspects of his personality that would later come to the fore.

In the late 1950s, after serving his sentence, Manson was released from prison. However, his criminal tendencies persisted, and he quickly found himself back behind bars for various offenses. Despite his repeated brushes with the law, Manson's magnetic charm continued to attract followers and admirers.

It was during one of these prison stints that Manson met a woman named Rosalie Jean Willis, whom he later married. Rosalie became pregnant, but their marriage soon fell apart, leading Manson to desert his wife and child.

The cycle of criminal behavior, imprisonment, and failed relationships further fueled Manson's growing disillusionment with society. The events of his early life laid the foundation for the emergence of a deeply disturbed and manipulative individual, whose charisma and twisted ideology would eventually lead to the formation of the notorious Manson Family and the dark chapter that would unfold in American history.

Chapter 2: Life of Crime Before the Manson Family

After his release from prison in the late 1950s, Charles Manson's life became deeply entwined with a series of petty crimes that continued to land him behind bars. Manson's early experiences with criminal behavior and imprisonment had not deterred him from a life of lawlessness; instead, they seemed to reinforce his criminal identity.

In the years following his release, Manson engaged in various petty criminal activities to sustain himself financially. These crimes included car theft, burglary, and check forgery. He roamed from city to city, eluding law enforcement and seeking new opportunities to feed his criminal tendencies.

Manson's criminal endeavors often revolved around living on the fringes of society. He associated with other delinquents and small-time criminals, forming alliances that provided both a sense of camaraderie and a means to commit further crimes. This period of his life was marked by a transient existence, moving from place to place to avoid capture.

However, Manson's penchant for trouble eventually caught up with him, leading to numerous arrests and incarcerations. He spent a considerable amount of time in various correctional institutions, including jails and prisons, as a result of his criminal activities.

During his time in prison, Manson's manipulative and charismatic nature began to attract a following of fellow inmates who were fascinated by his persona and stories of his criminal exploits. This early display of leadership over others hinted at Manson's future role as a cult leader.

Despite his time behind bars, Manson seemed undeterred by the prospect of facing the consequences of his actions. Instead, his criminal background appeared to fuel his desire for notoriety and a sense of superiority over society.

Manson's involvement in petty crimes and repeated incarcerations foreshadowed the emergence of a figure deeply entrenched in a criminal lifestyle. Little did the world know that this troubled and charismatic individual would go on to form a cult that would commit one of the most infamous and shocking crime sprees in history.

During his various stints in prison, Charles Manson honed his manipulative skills and further solidified his criminal connections. Prison provided him with a captive audience, and he used his charm and charisma to gain the admiration and loyalty of fellow inmates.

Manson's ability to captivate others and his penchant for storytelling made him stand out in the often brutal and competitive prison environment. He regaled his fellow inmates with tales of his criminal exploits, cultivating an image of a cunning and fearless outlaw. His stories, whether entirely true or exaggerated, garnered him a level of respect among his peers.

While incarcerated, Manson also developed a keen interest in various religious and philosophical texts. He delved into works by authors such as Dale Carnegie, L. Ron Hubbard, and Friedrich Nietzsche, drawing from their teachings to shape his own worldview. These readings, combined with his natural charisma, allowed Manson to create a pseudo-spiritual persona that would later play a central role in the formation of the Manson Family.

Additionally, prison proved to be a networking ground for Manson, where he established connections with like-minded criminals and individuals who would later become part of his inner circle. These connections would prove crucial in shaping the trajectory of his criminal ambitions.

Upon his release from prison, Manson continued to engage in criminal activities and established himself as a guru-like figure, attracting a group of followers who were mesmerized by his aura of mystique and supposed insights into the human psyche. The seeds of the Manson Family were sown during this time, as these followers became the first core members of his cult.

Through his experiences in prison and the associations he formed, Manson laid the groundwork for a criminal enterprise that would go beyond mere petty crimes. He was gradually building a network of devoted individuals who would eventually carry out his sinister and violent commands, leading to the darkest chapter in his life and American criminal history.

The formation of the Manson Family marked a pivotal moment in Charles Manson's criminal trajectory. Manson had become adept at manipulating others and weaving together a grandiose ideology that would serve as the foundation for his cult.

The early members of the Manson Family were mostly young, disenchanted individuals who were seeking meaning and purpose in a society undergoing significant social and cultural changes. Manson's charismatic personality and pseudo-spiritual teachings appealed to their desire for belonging and a sense of identity.

Central to Manson's ideology was his twisted interpretation of The Beatles' song "Helter Skelter." He believed that the song's lyrics foretold an impending race war between blacks and whites. Manson convinced his followers that they were destined to be the initiators of this apocalyptic event, which would result in the destruction of existing societal norms and power structures.

Under the influence of Manson's manipulative tactics, the members of the Manson Family became increasingly devoted and unquestioningly loyal to their leader. Manson exercised total control over his followers' lives, dictating their actions, beliefs, and even their sexual relationships. He often used a combination of drugs, sleep deprivation, and emotional manipulation to break down their individuality and create a collective, subservient group mentality.

The Manson Family established a commune at the Spahn Ranch, a dilapidated movie set in the California desert, where they lived an isolated and insular existence. Manson exploited the communal living environment to further indoctrinate his followers and prepare them for the impending Helter Skelter race war.

In an eerie display of commitment to his ideology, Manson orchestrated several acts of violence and vandalism to incite the race war he prophesied. The most infamous of these acts was the murder of Gary Hinman, a musician and acquaintance of Manson, in July 1969.

However, the true horror and notoriety of the Manson Family would be unveiled in August 1969 with the brutal Tate-LaBianca murders. The cult members carried out these heinous acts under Manson's explicit instructions, targeting the homes of actress Sharon Tate and supermarket executive Leno LaBianca. The vicious and senseless nature of the killings shocked the nation and catapulted Manson and his followers into the national spotlight.

The formation of the Manson Family and its twisted ideology paved the way for a series of horrific crimes that would forever stain the annals of American criminal history. The Tate-LaBianca murders would become one of the most chilling and notorious crime sprees in modern times, solidifying Charles Manson's legacy as an American cult leader and criminal mastermind.

Chapter 3: The Manson Family Cult

Central to the Manson Family's existence was Charles Manson's charismatic and manipulative personality. He possessed an uncanny ability to captivate and control others, drawing them into his web of influence. Manson's charisma was the driving force behind the formation and cohesion of the cult.

With his enigmatic aura and captivating storytelling, Manson had a unique way of attracting followers. He presented himself as a messianic figure, claiming to possess profound insights into human nature and the impending apocalypse. Manson's followers believed that he held the key to their salvation and the transformation of society.

Manson's charm extended beyond mere words; he was a charismatic performer and musician. He would often play the guitar and sing for his followers, using music as a tool to further manipulate their emotions and forge a deeper connection. His performances were hypnotic, leaving his audience entranced and vulnerable to his influence.

Under Manson's magnetic spell, many of his followers abandoned their former lives, including family, friends, and conventional societal norms, to join the Manson Family. He gave them a sense of belonging and purpose, promising them a life of communal harmony and spiritual awakening.

Manson fostered a deeply ingrained sense of dependency among his followers. He discouraged individuality and fostered a group mentality, wherein the collective will of the cult superseded that of the individual. This dynamic solidified his control over the group, as dissent or questioning of his teachings was not tolerated.

Through manipulation and psychological conditioning, Manson gradually stripped his followers of their sense of self and instilled in them a sense of devotion and unwavering loyalty. They became willing instruments, ready to carry out his orders, no matter how heinous or violent.

Manson's charisma was a potent force that bound the Manson Family together. His ability to inspire and manipulate his followers ultimately led to a level of control that allowed him to orchestrate the infamous Tate-LaBianca murders and other violent acts. The dark influence of Manson's magnetic personality would leave a lasting mark on the lives of his followers and the collective psyche of the nation.

Manson employed various recruitment methods to attract individuals into the fold of the Manson Family. His approach was particularly effective on vulnerable and impressionable young people who were seeking an alternative way of life and a sense of belonging.

One of the primary recruitment tactics was the use of communal living spaces, such as the Spahn Ranch, where Manson and his followers resided. The appeal of a close-knit community, free from societal norms and rules, enticed many individuals who felt alienated from mainstream society.

Manson's magnetic personality and charisma played a significant role in attracting potential followers. He had an innate ability to identify the vulnerabilities and desires of those he targeted, allowing him to tailor his message to resonate with each individual. He presented himself as a spiritual leader, offering the promise of enlightenment and salvation through his teachings.

Another aspect of Manson's recruitment strategy involved the use of hallucinogenic drugs, particularly LSD. He encouraged potential followers to partake in drug-induced experiences, claiming that such experiences would lead to heightened spiritual awareness and a deeper connection with the universe. These drug-fueled encounters were intended to break down barriers and increase susceptibility to his influence.

The Manson Family targeted those who felt disillusioned with mainstream society and sought an alternative lifestyle. Most of Manson's followers were young, disenchanted individuals who were often estranged from their families and lacked a sense of purpose. Many were runaways or had dropped out of school, seeking a sense of identity and community.

Most members of the Manson Family came from middle-class backgrounds, and several were college-educated, which challenged the notion that only disadvantaged or uneducated individuals could be susceptible to cult influence. Manson's manipulative tactics transcended social and educational boundaries, capturing the hearts and minds of individuals from diverse backgrounds.

The Manson Family members exhibited a wide range of personalities and characteristics. They were united by their devotion to Manson and their belief in the apocalyptic Helter Skelter ideology. Manson fostered a sense of family and camaraderie among his followers, which further strengthened their bonds and solidified their loyalty to him.

As the cult grew, Manson's ability to recruit and control new members became increasingly evident. The profile of the Manson Family members revealed the potent combination of Manson's manipulative skills and the vulnerabilities of those seeking a sense of purpose and community. It was this unique and dangerous mix that would set the stage for the horrific crimes that would soon shock the world.

Once individuals were drawn into the Manson Family, Manson employed a systematic process of indoctrination and brainwashing to solidify their loyalty and commitment to the cult's ideology. Manson's manipulative tactics were aimed at stripping away individual identity and creating a collective consciousness within the group.

At the core of Manson's indoctrination was the constant reinforcement of his own messianic status. He convinced his followers that he possessed divine insights and that they were chosen to play crucial roles in the impending Helter Skelter race war. He framed their actions as essential to initiating a new era of societal transformation and survival.

Manson discouraged any form of critical thinking or dissent within the cult. Questioning his teachings or expressing doubts was met with severe consequences, including emotional manipulation, isolation, and even physical punishment. He exerted absolute control over every aspect of his followers' lives, from their thoughts and beliefs to their daily routines.

To further cement the group's cohesion, Manson created an environment of fear and paranoia. He instilled the belief that society was against them, and that only by following his guidance could they survive the impending apocalyptic war. This sense of imminent danger and persecution heightened their dependency on him as their sole protector and leader.

Indoctrination sessions were often accompanied by drug use and prolonged periods of sleep deprivation. Manson used these techniques to weaken his followers' mental resistance and make them more receptive to his manipulations. The combination of drugs, sleeplessness, and relentless indoctrination sessions left the followers in a state of psychological vulnerability.

Manson also utilized the communal living environment to control his followers. He isolated them from the outside world and severed their ties with their families and friends. This isolation reinforced their reliance on the cult as their only source of emotional and social support.

Over time, Manson's followers became increasingly detached from reality, adopting his delusional worldview as their own. They saw him as a divine figure whose words were infallible and whose commands were unquestionable.

The process of indoctrination and brainwashing within the Manson Family transformed the initially diverse group of followers into a tightly knit, fanatically loyal, and unquestioningly obedient cult. Manson's manipulation of their beliefs and emotions set the stage for the horrific acts of violence that would follow, forever staining the Manson Family's name in infamy.

Chapter 4: Helter Skelter: The Apocalypse Vision

Central to Charles Manson's apocalyptic vision was his warped interpretation of The Beatles' song "Helter Skelter." Released in 1968 as part of The Beatles' self-titled album, commonly known as the "White Album," the song had a very different meaning from the one Manson assigned to it.

The original "Helter Skelter" was written by Paul McCartney and was inspired by a British amusement park slide of the same name. It was a lively and upbeat rock song with no overtly profound or violent messages. However, Manson, in his delusional state, perceived hidden messages within the song that confirmed his apocalyptic beliefs.

Manson believed that "Helter Skelter" was a coded message from The Beatles, intended for him and his followers. He thought that the song predicted a forthcoming apocalyptic race war between whites and blacks in America. According to Manson's twisted interpretation, the blacks would rise up and violently overthrow the white population, leading to the destruction of society as it was known.

Manson saw himself as the harbinger of this apocalyptic event. He believed that once the race war had decimated society, the Manson Family, who had taken refuge in a hidden underground city, would emerge as the new ruling elite. In Manson's deluded mind, this outcome was a necessary step towards a new era of peace and harmony.

To Manson, "Helter Skelter" represented a divine prophecy that confirmed his self-appointed role as a messianic figure. He saw his mission as preparing his followers for their central role in the impending race war. He believed that by committing a series of shocking and brutal murders, they could provoke the conflict that would lead to the fulfillment of his prophecy.

Manson used "Helter Skelter" as a rallying cry for his followers, convincing them that their actions were part of a grand cosmic plan. He used the song to manipulate and indoctrinate them, creating a sense of urgency and destiny that justified the atrocities they would later commit.

The twisted interpretation of "Helter Skelter" became the guiding principle of the Manson Family's actions. The song's innocuous lyrics transformed into a call for violence and chaos in the minds of Manson and his devoted followers, leading them down a path of horror and infamy that would forever be associated with their name.

Manson's apocalyptic vision centered on the belief in an impending race war that he referred to as "Helter Skelter." In his distorted worldview, this war was not merely a violent upheaval between different races, but a divine event destined to cleanse and transform society.

According to Manson, the Helter Skelter race war would be sparked by a racially motivated conflict between blacks and whites. He believed that African Americans would rise up against white oppressors, leading to widespread violence and chaos across the nation.

Manson's twisted ideology was rooted in a misinterpretation of social and political tensions of the time. The late 1960s were marked by civil rights struggles, protests against racial inequality, and growing divisions within American society. Manson exploited these real issues, projecting his delusional beliefs onto the existing social landscape.

He convinced his followers that they were chosen to be the initiators of Helter Skelter, and it was their divine duty to ignite the race war by committing a series of brutal and symbolic murders. The gruesome acts were intended to incite fear and chaos, creating an atmosphere of violence that would escalate into the predicted apocalyptic conflict.

In Manson's deranged vision, after the race war had run its course and society had collapsed, the Manson Family members would emerge from their hiding place and take control of the remnants of civilization. He believed that the Family would be the only ones prepared for the new world order, having undergone a process of spiritual purification under his guidance.

Manson's obsession with Helter Skelter drove him to plan and orchestrate the infamous Tate-LaBianca murders in August 1969. The horrific and senseless killings were intended to serve as a catalyst for the impending race war, according to Manson's distorted beliefs.

It is essential to recognize that Manson's apocalyptic vision was entirely based on his own delusions and manipulations. There was no basis in reality for his prophecy of Helter Skelter, and his violent acts were the result of a deeply disturbed mind and an insatiable desire for power and control.

The concept of Helter Skelter became the driving force behind the Manson Family's criminal actions, leading them down a path of destruction and violence that would reverberate through history and forever tarnish the name of Charles Manson and his followers.

Manson's obsession with the Helter Skelter ideology had a profound influence on the Manson Family's actions. His delusional beliefs and manipulative tactics led the followers to commit a series of brutal and senseless murders in an attempt to ignite the apocalyptic race war he envisioned.

The first act of violence driven by the Helter Skelter ideology was the murder of Gary Hinman in July 1969. Manson believed that Hinman's murder, which was committed by Manson Family member Bobby Beausoleil and others, would be blamed on African Americans, thereby inciting racial tension and violence.

However, it was the infamous Tate-LaBianca murders that catapulted the Manson Family into the national spotlight and solidified Manson's place as a cult leader and criminal mastermind. On the night of August 8, 1969, Manson ordered four of his followers – Charles "Tex" Watson, Susan Atkins, Patricia Krenwinkel, and Linda Kasabian – to carry out the brutal killings at the residence of actress Sharon Tate and her husband, director Roman Polanski.

The gruesome murders were intended to be a prelude to the Helter Skelter race war. Manson instructed his followers to leave behind signs that would frame the Black Panthers, a prominent African American civil rights group, for the crimes. He believed that this would escalate racial tensions and hasten the impending conflict.

The following night, August 9, 1969, Manson directed another group of followers – Watson, Atkins, Krenwinkel, and Leslie Van Houten – to carry out a similar brutal killing spree at the home of Leno and Rosemary LaBianca. Manson believed that these back-to-back gruesome murders would further fuel the race war narrative and trigger the societal chaos he desired.

The Manson Family's actions were fueled by a twisted belief system that justified violence and destruction as necessary steps toward an envisioned apocalypse. Manson manipulated his followers into committing these heinous acts under the guise of fulfilling a divine prophecy and playing pivotal roles in reshaping society.

The brutal Tate-LaBianca murders shocked the nation and led to an outpouring of public outrage and fear. The Manson Family's actions were seen as a horrifying reflection of the dark underbelly of the counterculture movement of the 1960s.

In the aftermath of the murders, Manson's apocalyptic ideology, and the cult's role in carrying out the atrocities, captured the attention of the media and the public. The Manson Family's connection to the Helter Skelter ideology became synonymous with mindless violence, brainwashing, and the dangers of charismatic cult leaders.

The Manson Family's actions were driven by a toxic combination of Manson's manipulative charisma and the distorted Helter Skelter ideology. The brutal murders stained the legacy of the counterculture era and became a cautionary tale of the devastating consequences of unchecked fanaticism and the dangers of following a charismatic but malevolent leader.

Chapter 5: The Spahn Ranch and Commune Life

After the gruesome Tate-LaBianca murders, the Manson Family went into hiding, evading law enforcement and public scrutiny. They found refuge at the Spahn Movie Ranch, a rundown former movie set located in the Santa Susana Mountains in California. The ranch was owned by George Spahn, an elderly man who allowed the Manson Family to stay on the property in exchange for doing odd jobs and chores.

The move to the Spahn Ranch marked a pivotal shift in the Manson Family's dynamics. The isolated and secluded nature of the ranch allowed Manson to further control and manipulate his followers without interference from the outside world. The commune lifestyle at the ranch intensified the group's cohesion, reinforcing their dependence on Manson as their sole leader and authority figure.

At the ranch, Manson maintained a carefully constructed hierarchy, with himself at the top. He surrounded himself with a small group of devoted followers who formed his inner circle, including individuals like Charles "Tex" Watson and Susan Atkins, who had participated in the Tate-LaBianca murders. These loyal followers held considerable influence over the other members of the Manson Family and helped enforce Manson's authority.

The communal living arrangement at the ranch meant that the Manson Family members shared living spaces, resources, and responsibilities. This arrangement not only fostered a sense of collective identity but also facilitated the enforcement of Manson's control over every aspect of their lives.

Manson continued to exert his manipulative tactics and used fear and intimidation to maintain his hold on the group. Any dissent or questioning of his authority was met with harsh punishments and isolation from the rest of the commune.

Living conditions at the Spahn Ranch were far from ideal. The property was run-down, and the Manson Family members lived in squalid conditions, often without adequate food, water, or sanitation. However, Manson convinced his followers that the difficult living conditions were part of their spiritual purification and preparation for the impending Helter Skelter.

The commune lifestyle at the ranch also facilitated the ongoing indoctrination of new members. Manson continued to recruit individuals, especially young women, who were drawn to the allure of the counterculture and Manson's charismatic persona. He manipulated their vulnerabilities and desires for belonging, quickly integrating them into the cult and making them part of his devoted following.

The relocation to the Spahn Ranch and the adoption of a commune lifestyle provided Manson with an environment conducive to maintaining control over his followers and furthering his apocalyptic vision. The ranch became the center of the Manson Family's operations, from planning their next actions to rehearsing their future roles in the impending race war. The secluded and insulated nature of the commune allowed the dark influence of Manson to take root and flourish, leading to further acts of violence and terror.

The Manson Family's relocation to the Spahn Ranch brought about a radical transformation in their way of life. The commune lifestyle at the ranch allowed Manson to solidify his control over his followers and perpetuate the atmosphere of subservience and loyalty that characterized the cult.

At the Spahn Ranch, Manson established a strict hierarchical structure, with himself at the pinnacle as the unquestionable leader and authority figure. He demanded absolute obedience from his followers and used fear and manipulation to maintain their allegiance. Those who demonstrated complete devotion to him were rewarded with his favor and trust, while any sign of rebellion or doubt was met with severe punishment.

Manson's inner circle, consisting of his most loyal and trusted followers, played a crucial role in enforcing his authority over the rest of the commune. They acted as enforcers, ensuring that Manson's directives were carried out without question and that dissent was swiftly quashed. Among the key members of Manson's inner circle were Charles "Tex" Watson, Susan Atkins, Patricia Krenwinkel, and Leslie Van Houten, who were directly involved in the Tate-LaBianca murders.

The communal living arrangement at the ranch further reinforced the cult's collective identity. Manson fostered a sense of family and camaraderie among his followers, encouraging them to see each other as brothers and sisters in the Manson Family. This tight-knit community mentality served to strengthen their loyalty to Manson and discouraged any form of individuality or independence.

Manson continued to exploit the vulnerability and naivety of new recruits, often young women drawn to the counterculture movement and the allure of Manson's persona. He subjected them to a process of indoctrination and manipulation, breaking down their sense of self and reshaping their beliefs to align with his apocalyptic ideology.

The communal living conditions at the ranch were far from ideal. The Manson Family members lived in crowded and squalid conditions, often sleeping in makeshift shelters and surviving on meager rations. However, Manson convinced his followers that their sacrifices were necessary for their spiritual growth and preparation for Helter Skelter.

Within the ranch, Manson controlled access to information from the outside world. He limited communication with family and friends, cutting off his followers from any potential outside influence that might challenge his authority or beliefs. This isolation further strengthened the bonds between the Manson Family members and intensified their dependence on Manson for guidance and validation.

The Spahn Ranch became a breeding ground for the dark and malevolent influence of Manson's charismatic personality. The commune dynamics and hierarchical structure allowed him to create an environment of fear, control, and devotion that fueled the cult's continued criminal activities and set the stage for the further horrors that would follow.

As the Manson Family settled into their new life at the Spahn Ranch, Manson's paranoia and obsession with the Helter Skelter ideology reached alarming heights. He became increasingly convinced that the race war he prophesied was imminent, and he pushed his followers to prepare for this perceived apocalypse.

Manson's escalating paranoia was fueled by a combination of factors. He believed that law enforcement agencies were closing in on the Family for their involvement in the Tate-LaBianca murders. To avoid capture, Manson led the Family through a series of relocations and hiding places, further isolating them from the outside world.

Within the ranch, Manson intensified his control over his followers, subjecting them to stricter discipline and a regimented daily routine. He enforced a sense of urgency, warning that the Helter Skelter race war was just around the corner and that they must be prepared to act when the time came.

The Manson Family members spent hours each day practicing weapons handling and combat training. Manson believed that they needed to be skilled fighters to survive the impending war and secure their place as the ruling elite after the chaos subsided. The constant drills and martial training served to further reinforce the cult's collective identity and strengthen their bonds of loyalty to Manson.

Manson also stockpiled weapons and supplies, preparing for what he saw as an inevitable conflict. He encouraged his followers to view themselves as soldiers on a divine mission, ready to carry out his orders without hesitation. The fear of impending violence and chaos served to solidify Manson's control over the Family, as they saw him as their only source of protection and guidance in the tumultuous times to come.

Despite the mounting tensions and paranoia, Manson continued to manipulate his followers with promises of salvation and spiritual awakening. He presented the impending Helter Skelter as a necessary and transformative event, convincing them that they were destined to play crucial roles in reshaping the world.

Manson's obsession with the Helter Skelter ideology and his relentless indoctrination efforts contributed to an atmosphere of desperation and fanaticism within the Family. The followers were willing to do whatever it took to fulfill Manson's vision, even if it meant committing further acts of violence and terror.

The Spahn Ranch became a pressure cooker of fear, manipulation, and distorted beliefs, with Manson at the center, controlling and shaping the minds of his devoted followers. The cult's escalating paranoia and preparation for the perceived impending war would eventually lead to further acts of brutality, culminating in a shocking and tragic event that would further solidify the Manson Family's place in history as a dark and malevolent force.

Chapter 6: The Notorious Tate-LaBianca Murders

The Tate-LaBianca murders, which occurred in August 1969, are the most infamous and chilling crimes associated with the Manson Family. The murders were meticulously planned and executed under Charles Manson's direction, with the intent of inciting the apocalyptic race war he called "Helter Skelter."

On the night of August 8, 1969, Manson instructed four of his followers – Charles "Tex" Watson, Susan Atkins, Patricia Krenwinkel, and Linda Kasabian – to carry out the first round of murders at the residence of actress Sharon Tate and her husband, director Roman Polanski. At the time, Tate was eight and a half months pregnant.

Armed with knives and firearms, the Manson Family members entered the Tate residence while the occupants were sleeping. They brutally attacked and killed Sharon Tate and four others who were present that night: Jay Sebring, a celebrity hairstylist; Voytek Frykowski, a close friend of Polanski; Abigail Folger, an heiress and Frykowski's girlfriend; and Steven Parent, a friend of the estate's caretaker.

The Tate murders were exceptionally brutal, marked by extreme violence and overkill. The victims were bound, tortured, and stabbed multiple times. The word "PIG" was scrawled in blood on the front door, with Manson hoping to incite public outrage by framing the Black Panthers for the murders.

The following night, August 9, 1969, Manson directed another group of followers – Watson, Atkins, Krenwinkel, and Leslie Van Houten – to carry out a similar brutal killing spree at the home of Leno and Rosemary LaBianca. The couple was bound and stabbed to death, and once again,

Manson hoped to leave clues pointing towards the involvement of African Americans in the crimes.

The Tate-LaBianca murders sent shockwaves through the nation, shocking the public with their senseless brutality and the apparent randomness of the victims. The Hollywood connection to the murders, with Sharon Tate being a prominent actress, further heightened media attention and public interest.

The Manson Family's involvement in the murders remained unknown for some time, but they continued to live in hiding, evading law enforcement and public scrutiny. It was only in October 1969 that the Family was arrested on unrelated charges, and evidence linking them to the Tate-LaBianca murders was eventually uncovered.

The infamous murders and the subsequent trial of Manson and his followers captivated the nation and left an indelible mark on American society. The shocking brutality and Manson's charismatic manipulation of his followers showcased the dangers of unchecked cult influence and the capacity for evil within seemingly ordinary individuals. The Tate-LaBianca murders would forever be remembered as one of the darkest chapters in American criminal history.

The Tate-LaBianca murders were marked by horrifying brutality, with the victims subjected to unimaginable violence at the hands of Manson Family members under Charles Manson's orders.

On the night of August 8, 1969, four Manson Family members entered the home of actress Sharon Tate and her husband, director Roman Polanski, in the upscale neighborhood of Benedict Canyon, Los Angeles. The victims present that night were Sharon Tate, who was eight and a half months pregnant, Jay Sebring, a celebrity hairstylist and close friend of Tate's, Voytek Frykowski, a writer and friend of Polanski, Abigail

Folger, an heiress and Frykowski's girlfriend, and Steven Parent, a friend of the estate's caretaker.

The Manson Family members, armed with knives and firearms, first encountered Steven Parent, who was in his car outside the residence. They shot and killed him before proceeding inside the house. Inside, they brutally attacked and murdered the other occupants.

Sharon Tate, Jay Sebring, and Voytek Frykowski were bound and stabbed multiple times. Sharon Tate pleaded for the life of her unborn child, but her pleas were ignored, and she was brutally killed. The attackers showed no mercy, inflicting horrific injuries on the victims. The level of violence and overkill was shocking and became a hallmark of the Manson Family's heinous acts.

Abigail Folger attempted to escape but was chased down and repeatedly stabbed by Susan Atkins. The killers then moved on to Jay Sebring, who was bound and shot. Voytek Frykowski fought desperately for his life, managing to break free momentarily, but he was eventually subdued and brutally murdered.

The word "PIG" was written in blood on the front door, in an attempt to frame the Black Panthers for the murders. This was part of Manson's twisted plan to incite racial tensions and spark the Helter Skelter race war.

The following night, August 9, 1969, another group of Manson Family members carried out a similar brutal killing spree at the home of Leno and Rosemary LaBianca. The couple was tied up and stabbed to death, with the attackers again leaving behind messages intended to implicate other parties.

The Tate-LaBianca murders sent shockwaves through society, terrifying the public with the senseless and brutal nature of the crimes. The victims were innocent people, chosen seemingly at random, and their deaths were carried out in the most sadistic and savage manner.

The Manson Family's callous disregard for human life and the monstrous details of the killings shocked the nation, leaving a lasting impact on American culture and criminal history. The horrific events of those two nights and the subsequent trial would forever stain the legacy of Charles Manson and his followers.

The Tate-LaBianca murders sparked a wave of public outrage and fear across the nation. The shocking brutality of the crimes, combined with the seemingly random and high-profile nature of the victims, sent shockwaves through American society.

News of the murders dominated headlines, and the media frenzy surrounding the case intensified when it became apparent that the killings were not isolated incidents. The bizarre and sinister details that emerged during the investigation, including the cult connections and Manson's apocalyptic ideology, captivated the public's imagination and horrified the nation.

The brutal killings at Sharon Tate's residence, a prominent actress and a symbol of Hollywood glamour, struck a chord with the public, further heightening the media's interest in the case. The link to the counterculture movement and Manson's manipulation of vulnerable young followers raised concerns about the dangers of cult influence and the potential for violence among seemingly ordinary individuals.

The Manson Family's involvement in the murders became a subject of intense speculation, with various theories and rumors circulating in the media. The revelation of Manson's twisted Helter Skelter ideology added another layer of complexity to the case, making it a chilling cautionary tale of the dark side of the counterculture movement and the dangers of charismatic cult leaders.

The media's portrayal of Manson as a deranged and evil mastermind played a significant role in shaping public perception. The iconic image of Manson with his wild eyes and a swastika carved into his forehead became a symbol of malevolence and madness. His courtroom antics and bizarre behavior during the trial only served to reinforce the public's perception of him as a dangerous and unhinged criminal.

Public fascination with the case reached a fever pitch during Manson's trial, which began in June 1970. The courtroom proceedings were a spectacle, with Manson frequently disrupting the trial and showcasing his defiance against authority. The media closely covered every aspect of the trial, contributing to the enduring notoriety of Manson and his followers.

As the trial progressed, Manson's control over his followers began to wane. Some of his devoted followers, who had once been willing to carry out his every command, began to turn against him, testifying against him in court. Manson's once tight-knit Family started to fracture under the weight of the evidence and the realization of the monstrous acts they had committed.

The public's morbid fascination with the Manson Family and their heinous crimes continued long after the trial. Books, documentaries, and movies about the case proliferated, solidifying Manson's place in pop culture as an infamous criminal mastermind. The Tate-LaBianca murders would forever be etched in the collective memory of society, serving as a haunting reminder of the dark potential that lies within the human psyche.

Chapter 7: Manson's Trial and Infamous Courtroom Behavior

The trial of Charles Manson and his followers began on June 15, 1970, in Los Angeles. Manson, along with Susan Atkins, Patricia Krenwinkel, and Leslie Van Houten, faced charges of murder and conspiracy for their involvement in the Tate-LaBianca murders. Charles "Tex" Watson, who had also been arrested, was tried separately due to a change in California's death penalty laws.

The trial garnered intense media coverage and public interest, with journalists and spectators flocking to the courthouse to witness the proceedings. Manson's charismatic and defiant demeanor during the trial, combined with the shocking nature of the crimes, made the case a media sensation.

From the outset, Manson used the trial as a platform to promote his apocalyptic ideology and to exert control over his followers who were still in the courtroom. He carved an "X" into his forehead, later changing it to a swastika, as a sign of his dissociation from society and to symbolize his status as an "ex-convict" in the eyes of the law. His followers, most notably Susan Atkins, mimicked his actions and carved "X"s into their foreheads as well.

Manson's courtroom behavior was marked by theatrical antics and attempts to disrupt the proceedings. He frequently interrupted the trial with outbursts, attempted to attack the judge, and even sang songs in court. His actions were part of a deliberate effort to control the narrative and maintain his image as a defiant and messianic figure.

Manson's followers also displayed unwavering loyalty to him during the trial. They openly declared their allegiance and devotion to him, even singing songs inspired by his teachings. Their behavior, combined with

Manson's manipulative control over them, further fascinated and horrified the public and the media.

As the trial progressed, Manson's defense team attempted to portray him as a misunderstood and charismatic figure rather than a criminal mastermind. They argued that Manson did not directly participate in the murders and should not be held responsible for the actions of his followers.

The prosecution, however, presented compelling evidence linking Manson to the murders, including witness testimonies from former cult members who had turned against him and cooperated with law enforcement. These testimonies shed light on the cult's brainwashing and Manson's role in orchestrating the crimes.

On January 25, 1971, after a lengthy trial, Manson, Atkins, Krenwinkel, and Van Houten were found guilty of multiple counts of murder and conspiracy. They were sentenced to death. Charles "Tex" Watson, who was tried separately, was also found guilty and received the death penalty.

The trial of Charles Manson and his followers was one of the most high-profile and infamous criminal cases in American history. It showcased the dangers of cult influence and the devastating consequences of unchecked fanaticism. Manson's manipulative control over his followers, combined with the shocking brutality of the crimes, left an indelible mark on the collective consciousness of society.

Throughout the trial, Charles Manson's behavior in the courtroom continued to be bizarre, disruptive, and calculated to manipulate both the proceedings and public perception. Manson saw the trial as an opportunity to further his apocalyptic ideology and to exert control over his followers, who were still present in the courtroom.

Manson often used the trial as a stage to espouse his delusional beliefs and to present himself as a messianic figure. He sought to maintain an aura of mystery and power, playing up his role as a misunderstood and charismatic leader rather than a criminal mastermind.

One of Manson's infamous courtroom antics was when he carved an "X" into his forehead, which he later transformed into a swastika. Manson claimed that the "X" represented his status as an "ex-convict" in the eyes of society and his rejection of the establishment. The swastika, though universally associated with hate and racism, was, in Manson's twisted view, a symbol of his defiance against societal norms.

Manson's followers, most notably Susan Atkins, Leslie Van Houten, and Patricia Krenwinkel, followed his lead and carved "X"s into their foreheads as well. This act of solidarity demonstrated their unwavering loyalty to Manson and their adherence to his ideology.

The disruptive behavior continued throughout the trial, with Manson attempting to attack the judge on one occasion and being forcibly removed from the courtroom multiple times due to his outbursts. He would interrupt proceedings with incoherent ramblings and nonsensical statements, often chanting phrases from his Helter Skelter ideology.

Manson's theatrical actions were part of a strategy to control the narrative and maintain his image as a defiant and enigmatic figure. He reveled in the attention and manipulation, believing that he could influence public opinion and garner support for his cause.

Despite his disruptive behavior, Manson remained a magnetic and mesmerizing presence in the courtroom. His followers continued to view him as their leader and spiritual guide, seemingly unshaken by the damning evidence presented against him.

The trial was not only a spectacle for the media and the public but also a harrowing experience for the victims' families and loved ones who had to endure the painful details of the murders and witness Manson's defiant behavior.

On March 29, 1971, the jury recommended the death penalty for Manson, Atkins, Krenwinkel, and Van Houten. The sentence was later commuted to life in prison when California temporarily abolished the death penalty in 1972. Charles "Tex" Watson, who was tried separately, was also sentenced to death.

Manson's trial and his courtroom antics cemented his place as one of the most notorious and chilling criminals in American history. His manipulation and control over his followers, combined with the shocking brutality of the murders, left a lasting impact on the criminal justice system and societal perceptions of cults and their charismatic leaders.

The Manson Family trial had a profound impact on public opinion and the perception of cults in American society. The shocking details of the murders and Manson's manipulative control over his followers sparked widespread fear and fascination, leading to a reevaluation of the counterculture movement and the dangers of charismatic cult leaders.

The Manson trial brought to the forefront the dark side of the 1960s counterculture and its potential for violence. The era, often associated with peace, love, and nonconformity, was now viewed with more skepticism and concern. Manson's ability to manipulate vulnerable young individuals and turn them into cold-blooded killers shattered the romanticized image of the "hippie" movement.

The trial raised questions about the power of charismatic leaders to indoctrinate and brainwash followers into committing acts of violence. It became a cautionary tale about the dangers of unchecked fanaticism and the risks associated with blindly following a charismatic figure.

The Manson trial also shed light on the vulnerability of young individuals who seek belonging and acceptance within countercultural movements or cults. The case highlighted the importance of education and awareness regarding the tactics used by manipulative cult leaders to exploit and control their followers.

Additionally, the trial exposed the need for improved mechanisms to prevent and address cult involvement and the potential for violence. Law enforcement and society as a whole began to pay closer attention to emerging cults and organizations with potential for harmful activities.

The media's extensive coverage of the trial contributed to the public's fascination with cults and the psychology behind individuals who join and commit crimes on behalf of such groups. The trial also sparked interest in the study of coercive persuasion techniques and the psychology of cult dynamics.

The Manson Family trial had far-reaching consequences on public perceptions of cults and their charismatic leaders. It exposed the dark underbelly of these organizations, helping society recognize the importance of identifying and addressing the potential dangers they pose.

In the years following the trial, various government agencies and organizations developed programs and resources to educate the public about the signs of cult involvement and to provide support to those who may have been affected.

Ultimately, the Manson Family trial served as a wake-up call for American society, leading to increased awareness and vigilance regarding cults and the potential for violence and manipulation. It became a pivotal moment in understanding the complex dynamics of cults and their impact on individuals and society as a whole.

Chapter 8: Aftermath and Impact of the Manson Murders

After the conclusion of the trial, Charles Manson and his followers faced the consequences of their heinous crimes. On March 29, 1971, the jury recommended the death penalty for Manson, Susan Atkins, Patricia Krenwinkel, and Leslie Van Houten. Charles "Tex" Watson, who was tried separately, had already been sentenced to death earlier.

However, in 1972, the California Supreme Court abolished the death penalty, leading to the commutation of the Manson Family members' death sentences to life imprisonment. Manson, Atkins, Krenwinkel, and Van Houten were sentenced to life in prison without the possibility of parole.

Their life sentences marked the end of Manson's dreams of becoming a martyr and igniting the race war he had envisioned. Instead, he spent the rest of his life behind bars, confined to the California State Prison in Corcoran.

Manson's incarceration did not diminish his hold over some of his followers who were not involved in the murders. Despite his imprisonment, Manson continued to exert control over his loyal disciples through letters and occasional visits. His magnetic charisma and manipulative influence remained strong, leading to ongoing concerns about his potential to inspire violence even from behind bars.

Over the years, several members of the Manson Family were paroled, while others remained incarcerated for their roles in the murders. Susan Atkins, who had actively participated in the Tate-LaBianca killings, died of brain cancer while serving her life sentence in 2009. Patricia Krenwinkel and Leslie Van Houten continued to seek parole but were repeatedly denied due to the severity of their crimes.

Charles Manson's notoriety and influence extended beyond his own followers. His actions and the heinous nature of the murders left a lasting impact on American society, sparking fear and paranoia about cults and their potential for violence. The Manson Family's criminal acts became a cautionary tale about the dangers of unchecked fanaticism and the dark allure of charismatic leaders.

The Tate-LaBianca murders also had a profound effect on Hollywood and the entertainment industry. The killings shattered the illusion of Hollywood as a place of glamour and stardom, exposing its underbelly of darkness and crime.

In the decades that followed, Manson's legacy continued to loom large. He was the subject of numerous books, documentaries, and movies, contributing to his status as a notorious figure in popular culture. The fascination with Manson and his crimes endures to this day, highlighting the morbid curiosity that society holds for the darkest aspects of human behavior.

Charles Manson died on November 19, 2017, at the age of 83. Despite his death, his dark legacy and the impact of his crimes on American culture and criminal history continue to be subjects of study, debate, and reflection. The Manson Family's horrific actions serve as a grim reminder of the capacity for evil within the human psyche and the importance of understanding and confronting the dangers of manipulation and fanaticism.

The Manson murders had a profound and lasting impact on American society. The shocking brutality of the crimes and Manson's manipulation of his followers left the public in a state of fear and disbelief. People were forced to confront the dark and sinister underbelly of humanity, and the sense of safety and innocence that had once been associated with the counterculture movement was shattered.

The Tate-LaBianca murders were seen as symbolic of a broader breakdown of societal values and moral standards. The Manson Family's willingness to commit such horrific acts in the name of an apocalyptic ideology sent shockwaves through society, raising questions about the potential for evil and violence lurking beneath the surface of seemingly ordinary individuals.

The Manson murders also intensified public fear of cults and their charismatic leaders. Many people became wary of countercultural movements and alternative lifestyles, fearing that they might lead individuals down a dangerous path. The term "cult" took on a negative connotation, associated with brainwashing, violence, and blind obedience.

The media played a significant role in perpetuating public fear and fascination with cults and their leaders. Extensive coverage of the Manson Family trial, coupled with reports of other cult-related incidents, reinforced the idea that such groups posed a serious threat to society. This media attention also contributed to a surge of interest in true crime stories and cult-related documentaries, further fueling public anxiety.

In response to the Manson murders and the growing fear of cults, law enforcement agencies and organizations began to take a more proactive approach in monitoring and investigating cult activities. Educational programs and resources were developed to raise awareness about the signs of cult involvement and to provide support for those who may have been affected by cult manipulation.

The Manson murders also prompted discussions about criminal justice reform and the use of the death penalty. After the California Supreme Court abolished the death penalty in 1972, the Manson Family members' death sentences were commuted to life imprisonment. This decision reignited debates about the appropriateness and effectiveness of capital punishment in the United States.

The enduring fascination with the Manson case and its impact on public consciousness have continued for decades. Books, films, and documentaries based on the murders have been produced, keeping the story alive in popular culture and adding to the morbid curiosity surrounding the case.

Overall, the Manson murders left a deep and lasting scar on American society. The crimes highlighted the potential for violence and manipulation within cults and served as a grim reminder of the dangers posed by charismatic leaders who exploit vulnerable individuals. The shock and fear generated by the Manson Family's actions triggered significant societal changes and a heightened awareness of the potential for evil and darkness within the human psyche.

The Manson murders had a profound impact on American culture, leaving a lasting imprint on various forms of media and influencing how the Manson Family and its crimes were portrayed in books, movies, and documentaries.

In the aftermath of the trial, the Manson Family and Charles Manson himself became infamous cultural symbols of evil and depravity. Books detailing the Manson murders and Manson's life were published, many of them exploring the psychological aspects of the case and delving into the motivations behind the crimes. These books captivated readers and contributed to the public's morbid fascination with the dark and complex tale of the Manson Family.

The true crime genre, which explores real-life criminal cases and their perpetrators, experienced a surge in popularity following the Manson murders. The case set a precedent for the public's interest in understanding the minds of criminals and the inner workings of cults and extremist groups. True crime literature and documentaries that dissected the events leading up to the murders, as well as the trial and its aftermath, became bestsellers and garnered significant attention.

The entertainment industry also took inspiration from the Manson case. Numerous movies, both fictional and based on true events, were made about the Manson Family and their crimes. Some of these films attempted to explore the psychological complexities of Manson and his followers, while others focused on the shocking brutality of the murders. The cult leader himself, despite being in prison, became a cult figure in popular culture, often portrayed in various forms of media.

The Manson murders also left a lasting impact on Hollywood and its portrayal of violence in films. The brutal and senseless nature of the crimes, combined with their high-profile Hollywood connections, led to increased scrutiny and self-censorship within the film industry. Filmmakers became more cautious about depicting graphic violence in their works, mindful of the potential impact on society and public perception.

Additionally, Manson's apocalyptic ideology and the concept of Helter Skelter became part of the cultural lexicon. The phrase "Helter Skelter" is now often used to describe chaotic and disorderly situations. Manson's twisted interpretation of The Beatles' song forever changed the public's perception of the innocent lyrics, attaching a dark and sinister connotation to the iconic rock band's music.

The Manson case's cultural influence continues to resonate today, with new generations learning about the crimes through documentaries, podcasts, and various media platforms. The Manson Family remains a chilling reminder of the capacity for evil and manipulation within human nature.

While the Manson Family's crimes were undoubtedly horrific, their cultural impact provides an opportunity for society to reflect on the dangers of extremism, cults, and charismatic leaders. The legacy of the Manson murders serves as a sobering reminder of the complexities of human behavior and the need to remain vigilant against the dangers of blind fanaticism.

Chapter 9: Manson's Imprisonment and Later Years

Following his sentencing to life imprisonment, Charles Manson spent the rest of his life behind bars. He was incarcerated at various California state prisons, including San Quentin State Prison and Corcoran State Prison.

In prison, Manson continued to exert his manipulative influence over his followers who remained loyal to him. He received numerous letters from devoted followers and continued to communicate with them through correspondence. Despite his confinement, Manson managed to maintain a degree of control over his inner circle, inspiring fear and admiration from those who still believed in his twisted ideology.

Manson's charismatic persona and notoriety made him a target of fascination for other inmates and outsiders alike. He garnered a reputation as one of the most infamous and dangerous prisoners in the United States. This notoriety sometimes resulted in conflicts with fellow inmates seeking to test themselves against the infamous cult leader.

Throughout his imprisonment, Manson was involved in various incidents and disciplinary actions. He faced punishment for possessing contraband, violating prison rules, and engaging in confrontations with prison staff and other inmates. His behavior behind bars only served to reinforce his reputation as a defiant and dangerous criminal.

In addition to his encounters with other inmates, Manson received numerous requests for interviews and media appearances over the years. Journalists and filmmakers sought to gain insight into his mind and motivations, and Manson occasionally granted interviews. However, he often used these opportunities to manipulate the narrative, promoting his apocalyptic ideology and portraying himself as a misunderstood figure.

As the years passed, Manson's health declined. He suffered from various health issues, including heart problems, gastrointestinal bleeding, and respiratory ailments. He was hospitalized on multiple occasions for medical treatment.

Despite his health struggles, Manson's notoriety and influence continued to extend beyond the prison walls. He became a symbol of evil and madness in popular culture, and his image appeared in various forms of media, from documentaries to artwork and even merchandise.

While incarcerated, Manson never showed remorse for his actions or the pain he caused to his victims' families. Instead, he maintained his delusional and defiant demeanor, believing in the warped reality he had constructed.

Manson's life in prison and his interactions with other inmates remained a subject of fascination for the public and the media.

During his decades of imprisonment, Charles Manson made several attempts to secure parole. However, each attempt was met with resounding rejection by the parole board. Manson's notoriety, along with the severity of his crimes and his lack of remorse, made it clear to the authorities that he remained a significant threat to society.

Manson's parole hearings were also marked by his bizarre and defiant behavior, similar to what he displayed during his trial. He used these hearings as a platform to express his delusional beliefs and to maintain control over his followers, some of whom still believed in his apocalyptic ideology.

Despite Manson's incarceration, he managed to maintain a degree of influence over certain individuals who were drawn to his dark charisma.

He received numerous letters from admirers, some of whom sought to join his "family" or pledged their allegiance to him as devoted followers. These individuals, often seeking a sense of belonging or purpose, were vulnerable to Manson's manipulative tactics, even from a distance.

Although Manson was isolated from society in prison, his impact on his followers was evident in the actions of some individuals associated with his cult. Throughout the years, there were instances of criminal acts carried out by individuals claiming to be inspired by Manson or attempting to fulfill his twisted vision of Helter Skelter.

However, it is essential to note that the vast majority of Manson's followers had distanced themselves from him and renounced his ideology after the horrors of the Tate-LaBianca murders were revealed. Many former members of the Manson Family underwent a process of deprogramming and sought to move on from the dark chapter of their lives.

Despite his continued influence over a small group of followers and admirers, Manson's significance as a criminal mastermind had waned over the years. He no longer posed the imminent threat he once did during his active time as the leader of the Manson Family.

Manson's later years in prison were marked by declining health and various medical issues. He was frequently hospitalized for health complications, and his physical state deteriorated with age. However, even in his weakened state, Manson remained a symbol of evil and depravity for many.

On November 19, 2017, Charles Manson passed away at the age of 83 due to natural causes. His death marked the end of an era of terror and manipulation that had haunted the American consciousness for decades. Yet, the legacy of the Manson Family and their horrific crimes endures, continuing to serve as a stark reminder of the potential for evil and fanaticism in the human mind.

Following Charles Manson's death on November 19, 2017, at the age of 83, the world reacted with a mix of relief and morbid curiosity. Manson's passing marked the end of a dark chapter in American history, but his legacy as one of the most notorious criminals and cult leaders of all time endured.

News of Manson's death sparked renewed interest in the Manson Family and their crimes. Media outlets revisited the case, and various documentaries and retrospectives were produced to examine Manson's life, the crimes committed by his followers, and the lasting impact on society. The public's fascination with Manson remained evident, as evidenced by the surge in online searches and discussions about his life and the Manson Family.

In the aftermath of Manson's death, there were different reactions from those who had been affected by his actions. For the families of the victims of the Tate-LaBianca murders, Manson's passing brought a sense of closure, knowing that he would never be released from prison. However, for some individuals who had been under Manson's influence or were still devoted to his ideology, his death may have been viewed as the loss of a charismatic and revered figure.

Manson's death also raised questions about his enduring cultural impact and how society would remember him in the years to come. Some viewed him as a symbol of the dangers of unchecked charisma and the capacity for evil within the human psyche. Others saw him as a cautionary tale of the potential consequences of fanatical beliefs and the dangers of cults and extremist groups.

In the years following Manson's death, the fascination with his life and crimes continued to be a subject of exploration in various forms of media. Books, documentaries, and films continued to be produced, offering new perspectives and analyses of the Manson Family and its significance in American history.

Despite his death, Manson's dark influence did not completely disappear. His legacy lived on in the minds of those still captivated by his apocalyptic ideology and charisma. Some individuals continued to be drawn to the Manson mythos, keeping the legend alive through online forums, social media, and fringe subcultures.

The Manson case and its aftermath also served as a reminder of the ongoing challenges society faces in preventing and addressing the allure of charismatic leaders and the potential for violence within extremist groups. The Manson Family's actions highlighted the importance of understanding the psychological factors that lead individuals to join and commit crimes on behalf of such groups.

As time went on, Manson's notoriety evolved from the immediate public fear and fascination following the murders to a subject of historical study and cultural analysis. His life and crimes became a part of American criminal folklore, cautioning future generations about the dangers of manipulation, cult fanaticism, and the dark allure of charismatic leaders. The Manson Family's story remains an enduring and haunting reminder of the human capacity for both cruelty and resilience.

Chapter 10: Manson's Ongoing Legacy and Influence

Charles Manson's legacy continues to cast a long shadow over true crime and popular culture. Decades after his death, Manson remains an enduring figure of fascination and horror, leaving an indelible mark on various aspects of American society.

In the realm of true crime, the Manson murders and their aftermath are still among the most extensively studied and discussed criminal cases. Books, podcasts, and documentaries continue to delve into the intricacies of the crimes, the psychology of the Manson Family, and the social context in which these horrific events occurred. Manson's ability to manipulate vulnerable individuals and inspire violence remains a subject of fascination for researchers and criminal psychologists.

Manson's case also played a significant role in shaping public perceptions of cults, extremism, and charismatic leaders. The cautionary tale of the Manson Family serves as a stark reminder of the potential for violence and harm when individuals surrender their critical thinking to the influence of a charismatic figure. The case has contributed to the development of measures aimed at identifying and addressing the dangers posed by cults and extremist groups in society.

In popular culture, Manson's influence is evident in music, literature, film, and art. His dark charisma and apocalyptic ideology have inspired musicians, writers, and filmmakers who seek to explore themes of human psychology, society's dark underbelly, and the allure of evil. References to Manson and the Manson Family can be found in various songs, novels, and movies, reflecting the enduring impact of this disturbing chapter in American history.

Manson's image and iconography continue to be used as symbols of evil and counterculture rebellion. The image of Manson with his wild eyes and the swastika on his forehead has become synonymous with madness and malevolence. In subcultures and countercultural movements, Manson's image is sometimes employed to challenge societal norms and to represent a rejection of authority.

The internet and social media have further amplified Manson's influence, enabling fans and detractors alike to share information and perspectives about the Manson Family. Online communities and forums continue to discuss and debate the various aspects of Manson's life, his ideology, and the impact of the crimes.

It is important to note that while Manson's legacy persists, many people actively reject the glorification or romanticization of his actions and ideology. The continued interest in the Manson case also raises ethical considerations about how such infamous criminals should be remembered and represented in popular culture.

Overall, Charles Manson's enduring impact on true crime and popular culture serves as a reminder of the power of storytelling and the human fascination with the darker aspects of human nature. His life and crimes have become a cautionary tale about the dangers of unchecked fanaticism and the potential consequences of following charismatic leaders down a path of violence and destruction. The Manson Family's story remains a haunting and cautionary chapter in American history, challenging society to remain vigilant against the allure of evil and manipulation.

The Manson Family's crimes and Charles Manson's charismatic leadership have had a significant influence on other cult leaders and criminal organizations. While not all leaders or groups are as notorious as Manson, the tactics and ideologies employed by him and his followers have been emulated in various ways by other individuals and groups seeking to exert control over others.

Some individuals with narcissistic and sociopathic tendencies have drawn inspiration from Manson's manipulation techniques and methods of gaining devotion and loyalty from followers. These copycat figures may not commit the same level of violence as the Manson Family, but they exploit vulnerable individuals and establish their own cult-like structures of control and obedience.

Manson's twisted interpretation of The Beatles' song "Helter Skelter" as a call for an impending race war is an example of how cult leaders can distort popular culture and use it to promote their ideologies. This tactic has been observed in other cults and extremist groups that manipulate media and artistic works to justify their violent actions or recruit new followers.

The Manson Family's commune lifestyle at the Spahn Ranch, with its hierarchical structure and indoctrination methods, has also influenced other cults and criminal organizations. Some cults have adopted similar communal living arrangements and used isolation from the outside world to control their members and limit access to critical information.

Manson's ability to manipulate and brainwash his followers has left a lasting impression on the study of psychology and criminology. Researchers have examined the techniques employed by Manson and other cult leaders to better understand the mechanisms of mind control and coercion. This research has contributed to efforts to identify and intervene in potentially dangerous cults and extremist groups.

While Manson's impact on other cult leaders and criminal organizations is a concerning aspect of his legacy, it has also led to increased awareness and vigilance in identifying and addressing such threats. Law enforcement, mental health professionals, and communities have become more adept at recognizing the warning signs of cult involvement and potential violent acts.

In the wake of the Manson Family's crimes, society has become more proactive in addressing the dangers of extremist ideologies and the potential for violence in cult-like organizations. Awareness campaigns, educational initiatives, and resources have been developed to help individuals avoid falling prey to manipulative leaders and extremist ideologies.

The Manson case serves as a stark reminder of the need for ongoing vigilance against the allure of charismatic leaders who exploit vulnerable individuals for their own gain. Understanding the psychology of cults and the tactics employed by manipulative leaders is essential in preventing future tragedies and protecting individuals from falling victim to such influences.

The Manson Family's crimes and Charles Manson's enduring influence on true crime and pop culture have left a complex legacy. While his actions continue to captivate and horrify, they also serve as a cautionary tale about the dangers of blind fanaticism, manipulation, and the power of charismatic leaders to lead followers down a dark and destructive path. Society's ongoing vigilance and understanding of these factors remain crucial in safeguarding against the allure of evil and extremist ideologies.

The Manson Family's crimes and Charles Manson's disturbing ideology have left society with several crucial lessons that continue to resonate:

1. The Danger of Charismatic Manipulation: Manson's ability to captivate and control vulnerable individuals serves as a stark reminder of the dangers posed by charismatic leaders. The allure of such figures can lead people to commit heinous acts and follow destructive ideologies without question. Recognizing and understanding the tactics used by

manipulative leaders is essential in preventing others from falling under their influence.

2. The Threat of Extremist Ideologies: Manson's twisted interpretation of "Helter Skelter" and the ensuing violence demonstrated the potential consequences of extremist ideologies. His apocalyptic vision of a race war exemplifies the dangers of individuals adopting radical beliefs and using them to justify violent actions. Addressing and countering extremist ideologies remains an ongoing challenge for society.

3. The Importance of Recognizing Early Warning Signs: The Manson case underscores the importance of identifying and addressing warning signs of potential criminal behavior and involvement in cults. Early intervention, whether through education, mental health support, or law enforcement efforts, can be instrumental in preventing individuals from descending into violence and criminal activity.

4. The Impact of True Crime on Pop Culture: The Manson Family case marked a turning point in true crime's role within popular culture. The public's fascination with the case paved the way for an increased interest in exploring the psychology of criminals and the dynamics of cults and extremist groups. The responsible portrayal of such crimes in media and entertainment remains a challenge, as society grapples with the fine line between informative storytelling and sensationalism.

5. The Complexity of Human Nature: The Manson case serves as a chilling reminder of the dark and complex aspects of human nature. It illustrates the potential for both good and evil within individuals and highlights the need for ongoing efforts to understand and address the psychological factors that contribute to criminal behavior.

Ultimately, the Manson Family's actions and ideology serve as a haunting and cautionary tale. They remind us of the capacity for evil and manipulation within human society and the importance of remaining vigilant against extremist ideologies and the allure of charismatic leaders. The Manson case remains a somber reflection of the human condition, challenging us to confront the darkness that exists within ourselves and in society as a whole.

Don't miss out!

Visit the website below and you can sign up to receive emails whenever Scarlett Prescott publishes a new book. There's no charge and no obligation.

https://books2read.com/r/B-A-MWTZ-YRJMC

BOOKS2READ

Connecting independent readers to independent writers.

Also by Scarlett Prescott

Charles Manson (1934-2017) - An American Cult Leader and Criminal Mastermind
Cosmic Outlaws - The Legend of Bonnie and Clyde
Escobar's Shadow: The Complex Legacy of a Notorious Criminal
Ted Bundy (1946-1989) - Charming Evil: The Notorious Serial Killer of the 1970s